The Clarity Playbook

How Busy Professionals Can Think Better, Decide Faster, and Lead with Confidence

By

Rahul Goyal and Dr Huma Goyal

A HYPHNLabs Publishing

The Clarity Playbook

How Busy Professionals Can Think Better, Decide Faster, and Lead with Confidence

ISBN: 978-93-343-5372-3

Cover design by *Rahul Goyal.*

We dedicate this book to the exceptional mentors and leaders who have shaped our understanding of effective leadership and decision-making. Their wisdom, trust, and guidance enabled us to learn, experiment with, and implement the frameworks that form the foundation of this work.

To our parents and siblings, whose unwavering belief and encouragement fuel our continuous pursuit of excellence.

And to each other—as life partners and co-authors—for the endless support, late-night discussions, and shared commitment to helping others navigate complexity with clarity.

Prologue

The challenge hit us from two different directions, but the problem was identical: how do you make sense of overwhelming complexity when every decision matters?

Dr. Huma had completed her PhD from IIT Bombay and joined Hitachi R&D in Japan, working on renewable energy projects that could reshape how the world powers itself. Later, Rahul moved to Tokyo to launch Rakuten Mobile–Japan's ambitious fourth mobile network that would disrupt an entire industry. Different timing, different industries, same fundamental challenge.

In the fast-paced world of technology and innovation, we both witnessed something remarkable. While most teams struggled under pressure, constantly firefighting and making reactive decisions, certain leaders and their teams seemed to operate differently. They weren't working longer hours or using more advanced tools. Instead, they had something more powerful: clarity.

These high-performing teams consistently made better decisions faster. They navigated uncertainty with confidence. They turned complex problems into manageable solutions. Most importantly, they created environments where innovation thrived and team members felt empowered rather than overwhelmed.

The pattern became clear across industries over the years from telecommunications to renewable energy, from startups to global corporations. Success wasn't about having all the answers; it was about having the right frameworks to find those answers quickly and effectively.

As artificial intelligence (AI) transforms the modern workplace, these frameworks have become even more critical. The most successful professionals today don't fear AI disruption–they leverage it. They use proven decision-making structures to iterate faster, explore multiple solutions, and amplify their strategic thinking rather than replace it.

This book captures years of real-world application across different cultures, industries, and organisational structures. The frameworks inside have been tested in boardrooms in Tokyo, research labs in India, and innovation centres across the globe. They work because they're built on fundamental principles of human cognition and organisational behaviour, not trendy management fads.

Whether you're a project manager juggling multiple deadlines, a team lead navigating technical challenges, or an executive making strategic decisions, these tools will help you cut through complexity and lead with confidence.

Because in today's rapidly evolving business landscape, the ability to think clearly, decide quickly, and execute effectively isn't just valuable–it's essential.

Table of Contents

Prologue 5

Table of Contents 7

Introduction 9

Chapter 1: The 80/20 Reset 11

Chapter 2: The ABT Method 21

Chapter 3: The Pyramid Principle 31

Clarity Recap: Chapter 1-3 41

Chapter 4: The Eisenhower Matrix 43

Chapter 5: Calendar Design Thinking 51

Chapter 6: AI as a Thinking Partner 61

Clarity Recap: Chapter 4-6 73

Chapter 7: The Clarity Audit 75

Final Clarity Recap 83

Resources 87

Clarity Note Template 88

The Clarity Toolkit Checklist 89

About the Author 91

Introduction

Clarity isn't about knowing everything. It's about knowing what matters.

In my years mentoring startups, building teams, and writing online, I've seen one typical pattern: people don't burn out because they're lazy or unfocused. They burn out because they try to do *everything*.

That's why this book starts with the 80/20 Rule. It's the most straightforward yet most powerful tool for cutting through noise and doubling down on impact. Before you do more—let's first do less, better.

Chapter 1: The 80/20 Reset

"80% of outcomes come from 20% of efforts."

– Pareto Principle

Why Most People Misuse the 80/20 Rule

You've probably heard of the 80/20 Rule. It's everywhere in productivity books and business blogs.

But most people get it wrong.

They think it's a *nice-to-know* idea. Something theoretical. Or worse, they use it to justify cutting corners.

Here's the truth: The 80/20 Rule isn't about working less. It's about **working on what matters more**.

And when applied with intent, it can change how you plan, delegate, market, learn, and even rest.

What Is the 80/20 Rule?

Also called the Pareto Principle, the rule says that:

- 80% of results come from 20% of inputs
- 80% of revenue comes from 20% of clients
- 80% of happiness may come from 20% of habits

It's not always exactly 80/20—but the idea holds.

A **small number of things drive the majority of impact**.

If you don't pause to identify those things, you'll stay "busy" forever.

The Reset You Need

The modern knowledge worker is drowning in:

* Notifications
* Endless tools
* Meetings that feel important but aren't

This is where the 80/20 mindset becomes your filter.

You start asking:

What's the 20% that truly drives my outcome?

Examples:

* In your business: What are the 1-2 offers or services that bring 80% of revenue? Double down on those.
* In your writing: What 2 types of content drive the most shares or leads? Create more of that.
* In your Calendar: Which 2 meetings bring clarity or unblock others? Protect those–and drop the rest.

The reset isn't about doing less. It's about doing more of the *right stuff*.

Apply It in Your Daily Work

Let's make this practical.

→ Weekly Planning Filter

Before you start a new week:

- Write down your 5 most significant goals.
- Circle the top one or two that directly impact outcomes.
- Schedule time for those first.

→ Delegation Filter

Ask yourself:

> *"Is this part of the 80% that feels productive but doesn't drive growth?"*

If yes, automate, delegate, or delete it.

→ Reading / Learning Filter

You don't have to read 100 newsletters. Just 2 that make you think deeply.

→ Relationships Filter

Who are the 3-5 people in your life or network who bring insight, energy, or momentum? Invest more time there.

Example For Professionals

- **Project Managers**: Which 20% of tasks (e.g., risk planning, stakeholder alignment) prevent 80% of fire drills?
- **Marketing Leads**: What 2 campaigns drove 80% of leads last quarter? Reallocate budget there.
- **Software Engineers**: Which 20% of code improvements (e.g., performance optimisation) resolved 80% of bugs?

Case Study: How I Applied It

When I started writing newsletters and mentoring startups along with my day job, I was overwhelmed.

I tried, tweeting daily, posting on LinkedIn, responding to every comment, and running 1:1 meetings, building tools, and tweaking workflows. Guess what?

It wasn't sustainable. So, I did a 20-minute audit and:

- I looked at what content got me replies, shares, and actual conversation
- I noticed that long-form newsletter-style posts brought the best connections
- I realised most of my replies came from LinkedIn DMs - not Twitter

I cut Twitter. I doubled down on writing one clear newsletter every week. Result?

More clarity. More engagement. And more time to think.

A Powerful Question to Ask Weekly

> *"What's the one thing I could remove, delegate, or stop doing–and nothing would break?"*

What 3 tasks drive 80% of my outcomes this month? Use that question as a compass. Write it on a sticky note. Review it every Friday, or use below template.

YOUR 20% IDENTIFICATION EXERCISE

Task/Activity	Estimated % of outcome	Action (Double Down/ Delegate/Delete)
Task-1	[ ] %	[ ]
Task-2	[ ] %	[ ]
Task-3	[ ] %	[ ]
Task-4	[ ] %	[ ]
Task-5	[ ] %	[ ]

Instructions:

1. *List your top 5 tasks from last week*
2. *Estimate % contribution to key outcomes (revenue/clarity/growth)*
3. *Circle the 1-3 tasks driving ~80% of results*
4. *Commit to doubling down on these next week*

✓ ***Download checklist, tools and templates from https://rahulgoyal.co/resources/ or scan QR code below***

Wrap-Up: The Clarity Principle Behind 80/20

The goal isn't perfection. It's the focus.

The 80/20 Rule isn't a formula. It's a lens. One that helps you:

- Notice what matters
- Drop what doesn't
- And create breathing room for high-leverage work

In the next chapter, we'll explore ABT storytelling–a simple way to make your ideas stick.

But for now, pause.

Grab a pen.

Write down your 20%.

And reset.

Chapter 2: The ABT Method

"Facts don't persuade. Stories do."

– Seth Godin

Why Most Communication Falls Flat

You've likely faced this:

- ✳ You explain an idea, but it doesn't land.
- ✳ You pitch a product, and people nod–but don't act.
- ✳ You write a post, but no one replies.

It's not because your idea is weak.

It's because your message lacks structure.

That's where ABT comes in.

What Is ABT?

ABT stands for:

- ✳ **And**
- ✳ **But**
- ✳ **Therefore**

It's a storytelling framework created by scientist and filmmaker Randy Olson, rooted in how our brains process information.

Let's compare:

❌ Flat version:

> *"Our company makes eco-friendly packaging. It's recyclable. We care about the planet."*

✅ ABT version:

> *"Our company makes eco-friendly packaging, **AND** customers want sustainable choices, **BUT**, most packaging is still harmful to the environment, **THEREFORE**, we created a recyclable solution that saves waste and meets modern demand."*

Feel the difference?

The second one builds tension and resolution. That's what makes it sticky.

Why It Works

Humans are wired for stories.

Our brains look for:

- Context (AND)
- Conflict (BUT)
- Resolution (THEREFORE)

This framework works in:

- Elevator pitches
- Social media
- Emails
- Startup decks
- Leadership communication

Once you see it, you can't unsee it.

ABT in Real Life

Here's how you can use ABT right now:

➔ **For Your LinkedIn Bio**:

"I work with early-stage founders **AND** tech teams looking to scale fast, **BUT** they often hit roadblocks around clarity, direction, or hiring, **THEREFORE**, I help them design scalable systems that actually work."

➔ **For Product Copy**:

"Most photographers want to shoot more **AND** edit less, **BUT** pro tools are either expensive or confusing, **THEREFORE**, we built a lightweight app that's simple, powerful, and fast."

➔ **For Newsletter Writing:**

Start each edition with ABT:

- What's happening?
- What's broken?
- What's the new idea, lens, or takeaway?

This structure pulls the reader in.

Examples

Healthcare Worker:

*I treat patients **AND** want them to live healthier, **BUT** chronic conditions often stem from preventable habits, **THEREFORE** I focus on education that empowers daily choices.*

Teacher:

*I teach science **AND** students crave real-world connections, **BUT** curricula rarely link theories to practical applications, **THEREFORE** I design experiments using everyday materials.*

Engineer:

*We build software **AND** users want intuitive experiences, **BUT** complex requirements often create cluttered interfaces, **THEREFORE** we prototype with simplicity-first principles.*

Retail Manager:

My team stocks shelves AND customers want quick finds, BUT store layouts haven't changed with shopping patterns, THEREFORE we're testing data-driven zone redesigns.

ABT Template (Copy/Paste)

Use this anytime you're writing or explaining:

```
I/we do X AND [insert shared goal or belief],
BUT [insert the problem, gap, or friction],
THEREFORE [insert your solution, insight, or offer].
```

Want a shortcut?

💡 **Save it as a snippet in your notes app or ChatGPT custom prompt.**

ABT Workshop (Write Your Bio)

Rewrite your professional story in 10 minutes:

1. **AND (Context):**

   What you do + shared belief

   Example: "I help teams deliver complex projects"

   Your turn:

   [I/We do _____ AND _____]

2. **BUT (Conflict):**

   The obstacle your audience faces

   Example: "BUT most struggle with misaligned priorities"

   Your turn:

   [BUT _____]

3. **THEREFORE (Solution):**

   Your unique value

   Example: "THEREFORE I create clarity frameworks that cut noise"

   Your turn:

   [THEREFORE _______]

ABT Email Clinic

3 Ready-to-Use ABT Email Templates

1. **Sales Pitch Template**

Subject: *Solving [Pain Point]*

Hi [Name],

You're focused on [Goal] ***AND*** *want [Desired Outcome],*

BUT *I know [Specific Challenge] is slowing progress.*

THEREFORE *I'd like to share how [Your Solution] helped [Similar Client] achieve [Result].*

[Call-to-Action]?

2. Team Alignment Template

Subject: *Action Needed: [Project]*

Team,

We're launching [Project] ***AND*** *aligned on [Objective],*

BUT *timelines are at risk due to [Blockage].*

THEREFORE *let's meet [Time] to resolve [Specific Item].*

Bring: [Requirements]

3. Newsletter Hook Template

Subject: *Why [Topic] Isn't Working*

[First Name],

[Industry] talks about [Topic] ***AND*** *we all want [Benefit],*

BUT *most miss [Critical Gap].*

THEREFORE *this week's insight: [Provocative Takeaway].*

Read the full perspective ➔

✓ ***Download checklist, tools and templates from https://rahulgoyal.co/resources/ or scan QR code below***

Wrap-Up: The Clarity Principle Behind ABT

ABT makes your message clear and memorable.

Whether you pitch a product, write a tweet, or give feedback to a team, structure your message like a story–not a list.

Next, we'll explore a thinking framework used by strategy consultants and top communicators: the **Pyramid Principle**.

But first, try rewriting your LinkedIn or website intro using ABT.

You'll instantly stand out.

Chapter 3: The Pyramid Principle

"Effective communication is not about saying more. It's about saying what matters–first." – Barbara Minto

Why Clear Thinking Often Looks Like Clear Speaking

You've been there.

- A teammate shares an update... but you still don't know what they're asking for.
- A report is full of facts... but the conclusion is buried.
- You pitch your idea... and people say, "Interesting," but take no action.

The problem?

Unstructured thinking leads to unclear communication.

That's where the **Pyramid Principle** shines.

What Is the Pyramid Principle?

Created by **Barbara Minto**, a former McKinsey consultant, the Pyramid Principle is a simple but powerful way to structure your message.

At its core:

Start with the answer. Then, support it.

This is the opposite of how most people communicate (especially in business), where they build up slowly and bury the point.

With the Pyramid:

- Start with the main idea (the top)
- Group supporting ideas logically (the middle)
- Back them with data or examples (the base)

It's top-down thinking.

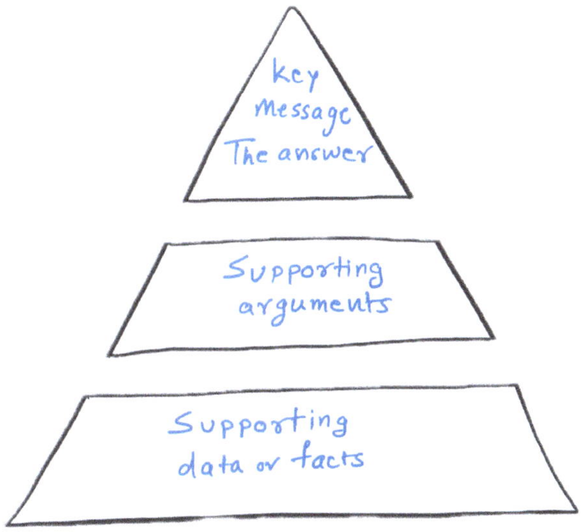

Why It Works

The human brain craves structure.

People don't have time to "get to the point." They need the point –first. That's why this model works so well in:

- Executive updates

- Emails
- Presentations
- Strategy documents
- Sales calls

It's not flashy. It's not creative writing.

It's just **clarity on demand**.

The Pyramid in Action

Let's say you're writing an email to your team about shifting project timelines.

❌ Most people write:

"We've been evaluating the roadmap, and after some discussion across teams and feedback from partners, we believe shifting the project by 3 weeks is the best decision..."

✅ **Pyramid version**:

Subject: Project timeline shifted by 3 weeks

Body:

We're moving the launch from July 3 to July 24.

Why:

- *The design team flagged a resource gap*
- *Our beta users asked for more testing time*

- *It aligns better with the marketing window*

Short, sharp, and clear.

How to Use It in Your Day-to-Day

➔ For Emails

- Start with the headline or outcome
- Add bullets for reasons
- Keep each level logically grouped

➔ For Presentations

- Begin with: "Here's the recommendation."
- Then, walk through the "why" with grouped support
- Save detailed data for appendices

➔ For Decision-Making

When you're stuck, build a pyramid on paper:

- Top: What's the decision?
- Middle: 2-3 key reasons
- Base: Any numbers, quotes, or examples

Use this to think before you speak or write.

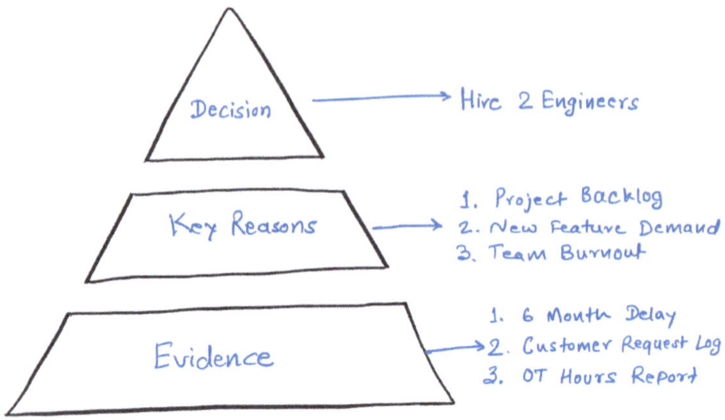

Examples

From Mentorship Session:

While mentoring a founder during summer 2024, she asked for feedback on her investor pitch.

It was 18 slides.

No one knew the "ask" until slide 16.

We **flipped** it using the Pyramid:

> *"We're raising £300K to grow from 50K to 250K ARR in 12 months."*

Then:

- Why us? (traction, team, tech)
- Why now? (market momentum, gaps)
- How? (clear use of funds)

That version led to multiple investor follow-ups—and clarity in every meeting.

Healthcare Director:

Top: "We need Telehealth expansion"

Middle:

1. 35% patient access barriers
2. Staff efficiency gains
3. Competitive parity

Base:

- Rural satisfaction survey
- Pilot program results
- Competitor launch analysis

Teacher Department Head:

Top: "Adopt project-based learning"

Middle:

1. Improves critical thinking
2. Aligns with new standards
3. Boosts engagement

Base:

- State assessment trends
- Student feedback
- Case study: Lincoln High

Retail Manager:

Top: "Extend holiday hours"

Middle:

1. 70% sales occur after 5pm
2. Competitors open later
3. Staff availability high

Base:

- POS throughput analysis
- Competitor hours audit
- Employee survey

Build the Habit

Here's a prompt you can use before writing or speaking:

🧠 **"What's my main point? Can I say it first–in one sentence?"**

Try this in:

- Meeting prep
- Newsletter intros
- Sales decks
- Client reports

Soon, it'll become second nature.

✓ ***Download checklist, tools and templates from https://rahulgoyal.co/resources/ or scan QR code below***

Wrap-Up: The Clarity Principle Behind the Pyramid

Clear thinking leads to confident communication.

The Pyramid Principle doesn't just make you a better writer–it makes you a better leader.

Next, we tackle **The Eisenhower Matrix**, a timeless tool to stop reacting and start leading.

Clarity Recap: Chapter 1-3

Chapter 1. The 80/20 Reset

- 20% of your efforts drive 80% of your outcomes.
- Identify high-leverage work and eliminate noise.
- Weekly question: "What can I remove or ignore–and nothing would break?"

Chapter 2. The ABT Method

- Use "And-But-Therefore" to shape clear, persuasive stories.
- It works for pitches, posts, bios, emails–anything.
- Structure = Stickiness.

Chapter 3. The Pyramid Principle

- Lead with the conclusion, not the background.
- Group supporting points logically, top-down.
- Especially powerful for decks, updates, and fast decisions.

🧠 **Checkpoint Prompt**:

> *"Am I doing fewer things, communicating better, and structuring clearly?"*

If yes–turn the page.

If not–bookmark this recap and come back next time you're stuck.

Chapter 4: The Eisenhower Matrix

"What is important is seldom urgent. And what is urgent is seldom important." – Dwight D. Eisenhower

Why We Work on the Wrong Things

You wake up. Check your phone.

Someone needs something. A fire's burning. A meeting just got moved. By 10 a.m., your plan is gone. And you're not alone. Most professionals spend their day reacting. Not thinking. Not deciding. Just responding.

The result?

Urgent work steals from important work.

But what if there was a map to escape that loop? That's where the Eisenhower Matrix comes in.

What Is the Eisenhower Matrix?

It's a 2x2 framework that helps you **prioritise work based on importance and urgency**.

	Urgent	**Not Urgent**
Important	DO (Now)	DECIDE (Schedule it)
Not Important	DELEGATE (If you can)	DELETE (Don't do it)

Named after U.S. President and military strategist **Dwight D. Eisenhower**, this tool helps leaders focus on strategy overreaction.

The 4 Quadrants

1. **Do First (Urgent + Important)**
   - Examples: critical bugs, urgent client issues, health emergencies
   - These are real fires. Handle them now–but don't live here.
2. **Schedule It (Not Urgent + Important)**
   - Examples: writing, strategy, learning, deep work, 1:1s
   - This is where great leaders spend time. Block it. Protect it.
3. **Delegate It (Urgent + Not Important)**
   - Examples: scheduling meetings, answering routine emails
   - Can someone else do it 80% as well? If yes–delegate.
4. **Delete It (Not Urgent + Not Important)**
   - Examples: mindless scrolling, unnecessary meetings, status updates
   - The trap zone. Looks like work. Isn't.

Most emails are urgent but not important. Use filters, autoresponders, or a VA. Don't be available 24/7–be useful when it counts.

How to Use the Matrix in Real Life

→ Daily Prioritisation

At the start of your day, write down your to-dos. Then, sort them into the matrix. Cross out 1-2 tasks immediately.

➔ Weekly Planning

Set aside 1 hour every Friday or Sunday. Ask:

> *"What important but non-urgent thing do I keep pushing off?"*

Schedule that first for the week ahead.

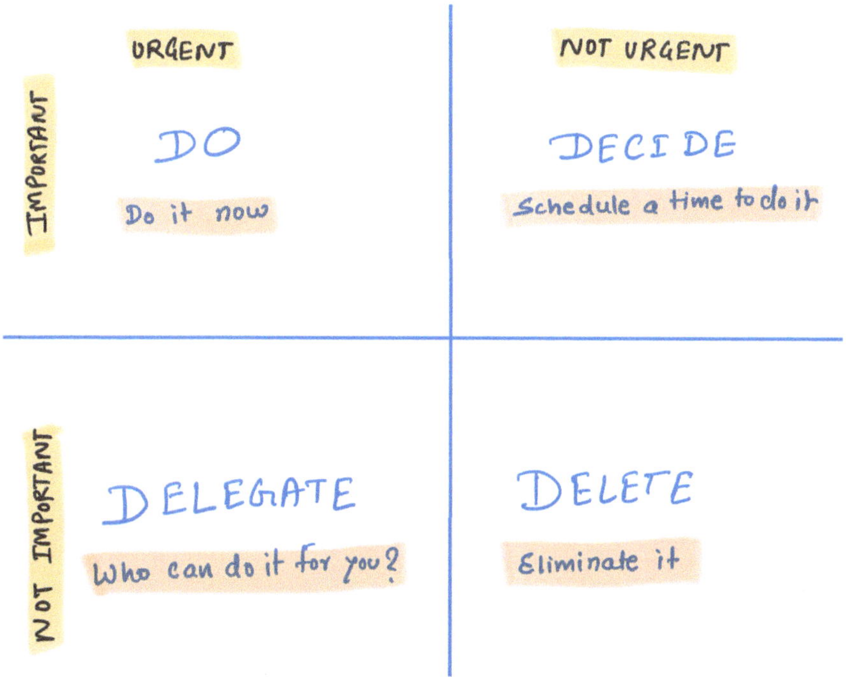

A Example

When I launched my second newsletter, I was also running a portfolio of projects. I was:

- Writing daily updates
- Replying to DMs
- Designing the website
- Testing 4 different tools

I was busy... but not effective.

So, I built a weekly Eisenhower board using sticky notes:

- Writing and publishing went into "Important, Not Urgent" ➔ blocked every Wednesday. (***now my Friday Purge ritual ensures these blocks stay protected!***)
- The automation setup -> delegated.
- New platform testing? Deleted.

That single reset freed up 6 hours a week.

More focus. Better output.

Friday Purge Ritual

Clear decision-clutter before the weekend:

1. **Dump Tasks:** List everything you did this week
2. **Categorize:**

[✓] DO (Urgent/Important): ___________

[ ] SCHEDULE (Important): ___________

[ ] DELEGATE (Urgent): ___________

[🗑️] DELETE (Neither): __________

3. **Action Plan**:

   - Delegate 1+ "Urgent/Not Important" task
   - Delete 2+ "Not Urgent" items permanently
   - Schedule 1 "Important/Not Urgent" for next week

Tip: *Do this with coffee at 4 PM Fridays - turns reflection into liberation.*

Build the Habit

Here's a quick way to lock this in:

🧠 At the start of each day, ask:

> *"Am I doing what's important–or just what's next?"*

If you're not sure, pause. Draw the matrix.

Sort your list. Then, act–intentionally.

✓ ***Download checklist, tools and templates from https://rahulgoyal.co/resources/ or scan QR code below***

Wrap-Up: The Clarity Principle Behind Prioritisation

You can't manage time. But you can manage focus.

The Eisenhower Matrix gives you a simple but powerful lens to stop reacting and start choosing.

In the next chapter, we'll explore a tool that brings your whole system together: Calendar Design Thinking.

Chapter 5: Calendar Design Thinking

"Show me your calendar, and I'll show you your priorities." – James Clear

How to Treat Your Calendar Like a Strategy Document

We often treat the Calendar as a *reactive tool*—a dumping ground for meetings, reminders, and events.

But what if we flipped it?

What if your Calendar became a **proactive strategy map**—a visual reflection of what actually matters to you?

That's the shift this chapter is about.

The Problem: Reactive Time ≠ Focused Energy

Most people manage their time like this:

- Accept every invite
- Cram in work-around meetings
- Leave "focus work" for when they're not tired (which rarely happens)
- End the week wondering: Where did all the time go?

They *use* a calendar but don't *design* one.

And that's the difference between operating in **default mode** vs **design mode**.

The Calendar Design Mindset

Think of your Calendar not just as a tool to manage time–but as a **canvas to design your attention**.

Start with this question:

"If I only had 20 hours per week to focus, what would I spend them on?"

You'll get immediate clarity on what matters.

From there, you work backwards–fitting everything else around those priorities.

Three Principles of Calendar Design

To move from chaos to clarity, build your week using these three principles:

1. Time Blocks > Task Lists

Tasks don't exist in isolation. They need **space**.

Instead of writing "Work on client pitch," block 90 minutes for it.

Instead of "Write a blog post," block 2 focused sessions.

🟩 Tip: Give blocks a verb + outcome

Example: "🧠 Plan Oct campaign (outline + slides)" – not just "Marketing."

Energy-Aware Blocking

Energy Zone	Urgent
Peak (Golden Hours)	Writing • Strategy • Creation
Moderate	Problem-solving • Planning • Learning
Low	Admin • Reviews • Routine task

Design blocks around your natural rhythm, not arbitrary timelines.

2. Theme Your Days

You don't need rigid routines. You need rhythm.

Assign soft themes to days of the week so your brain knows what kind of work to expect.

- Monday = Planning & Deep Work
- Tuesday = Meetings + Coaching
- Wednesday = Creation & Writing
- Thursday = Strategy & Thinking Time
- Friday = Buffer + Admin + Review

This reduces decision fatigue and keeps your momentum high.

3. Protect the Golden Hours

Everyone has 2-3 hours of peak creative energy daily.

For most, it's mornings. For some, it's late night.

🕒 Identify your "golden hours." Guard them like a CEO guards their board meeting.

- ✳ No meetings
- ✳ No context switching
- ✳ Just you and your most important work

Once you protect these hours, your week transforms.

When protecting golden hours, use this auto-response template:

> *"Thank you for your invitation! To protect my deep work blocks, I don't schedule meetings between [X AM] - [Y AM].*
>
> ➔ *Please reschedule via my Calendly or Outlook: [Link]*
>
> ➔ *For urgent matters: Text me at [Phone]*
>
> *I review requests at [Check Time] daily."*

Example: A Calendar in Design Mode

Here's what a "designed" calendar looks like:

Time	Block Description
8:00-10:00 AM	📘 Focus Work: Book Chapter Drafting
10:00-11:00 AM	🤝 Team Syncs (pre-scheduled)
11:00-1:00 PM	🔍 Deep Work: Proposal Review
2:00-4:00 PM	📞 External Calls / Coaching
4:00-5:00 PM	📁 Admin / Follow-ups / Cleanup

Every day has a **purpose**.

Every block has **intention**.

This is the essence of calendar design.

Tip: Add "Thinking Time" Every Week

Schedule at least one 60-90 minute block just for thinking.

No agenda. No laptop. Just a notepad or whiteboard.

Ask:

- What's working?
- What's broken?
- What's missing?
- What's next?

This one act alone will separate you from 95% of people running in circles.

Calendar Defence Tactics (Protecting Your Design)

1. The 24-Hour Buffer Rule

- All new requests wait 24hrs before acceptance
- Exception: True emergencies (<2% of cases)

2. The "Energy Tax" Test

Before accepting any meeting:

Will this:

[ ] Recharge my energy? ➔ *YES*

[ ] Drain my energy? ➔ *NO*

* *Study shows that high-performers decline 83% of "energy tax" events.*

✓ ***Download checklist, tools and templates from https://rahulgoyal.co/resources/ or scan QR code below***

Wrap-Up: The Clarity Principle Behind Your Calendar

Your Calendar = Your Strategy in Motion

Most strategy documents sit in drawers.

But your Calendar? You look at it every day.

It's the perfect place to **embed your focus**, **protect your energy**, and **move toward your goals** week by week.

Don't just use your Calendar. Design it.

Chapter 6: AI as a Thinking Partner

"The real power of AI isn't replacing your thinking. It's extending it."

We were promised flying cars. Instead, we got ChatGPT.

And surprisingly – that might be better.

AI today can't think *for* you. But it can absolutely think *with* you.

In this chapter, we'll shift the conversation away from hype and toward **practical clarity**:

How can AI become a tool that sharpens your thinking, not distracts it?

The Brain Problem

Here's the truth:

Your brain isn't built for storage.

It's built for **creativity, connections**, and **decisions**.

But most of us use our minds like messy desktops:

- Half-finished ideas
- Jumbled priorities
- Constant context switching

This mental clutter blocks clarity.

That's where the right AI tools come in—not to automate everything but to s**upport a higher-quality mental operating system**.

Don't Treat AI Like Google

Treat it like a Co-Worker

What is the biggest mistake people make?

They treat ChatGPT or other AI tools like a search engine:

> *"What is X?"*
>
> *"Give me 10 tips about Y."*

But the real unlock is this:

Use AI to organise your thinking, not just retrieve facts.

Imagine asking:

- "Here's my rough idea–help me structure it into 3 options."
- "Help me turn this messy outline into a clean summary."
- "What questions should I ask myself before making this decision?"

The more context you give, the smarter your AI partner becomes.

5 Ways to Use AI as a Thinking Partner

Here are five simple, strategic ways to start using AI daily:

1. Clarify Ideas

Use ChatGPT as a sounding board.

Paste your rough thoughts and ask:

"Can you simplify this in plain English?"

"What's the core message here?"

"Is this convincing or unclear?"

It won't always be perfect–but it will help you spot blind spots instantly.

2. Structure Before You Start

Before diving into a deck, article, or proposal, ask:

"Can you help me outline this logically?"

"What's the best structure for [audience] and [goal]?"

That's clarity before creativity.

3. Debrief Your Week

Use AI to reflect.

Paste a few bullet notes from your week:

"Summarise what worked vs didn't. Anything worth doubling down on?"

"Can you spot any patterns in my energy or focus?"

This isn't therapy. It's productivity hygiene.

4. Simplify Complex Stuff

Got something technical or messy?

Ask ChatGPT to:

> *"Explain this like I'm 12."*
>
> *"Turn this into a one-liner pitch."*
>
> *"Give me the pros/cons of these 3 ideas side-by-side."*

It's like having an intern who never sleeps.

5. Write to Think

Sometimes, typing to ChatGPT is thinking.

The back-and-forth helps you externalise thoughts faster than journaling.

Try it with:

> *"I feel stuck on this decision. Help me break it down."*
>
> *"Let's brainstorm–I'll give ideas, you expand."*

Think of it as a productivity partner that listens well and types fast.

Use with Boundaries

AI is powerful. But, like caffeine, it should be used intentionally.

Watch for these traps:

- **Over-relying**: AI should sharpen your judgment, not replace it.

- **Generic outputs:** If you don't bring clear context, you'll get bland advice.
- **Endless prompting**: Set time limits. AI is a tool–not a rabbit hole.

Use it to gain momentum, not escape decisions.

AI Rituals Framework

AI becomes powerful when embedded in routines, not used re-actively. These rituals create clarity muscle memory.

1. Morning Clarifier Ritual

When: First 10 minutes of workday

Prompt:

> *"Simplify today's priority: [Your goal].*
>
> *What's the core outcome?*
>
> *What could derail it?*
>
> *What's one question I should ask myself?"*

Samle output

> *Core: Finish investor deck.*
>
> *Risk: Over-designing slides.*
>
> *Question: 'Will this slide change their decision?*

2. Weekly Architect Session

When: Friday afternoons

Prompt:

Review my week:

Wins: [3 bullets with measurable outcome]

Struggles: [3 bullets with time/energy cost]

Patterns?

Next week's anchor task?

Samle Input

Wins:

Finished investor deck ➔ secured follow-up meeting

Delegated 5 admin tasks ➔ saved 3 hours

Ran team retrospective ➔ resolved workflow bottleneck

Struggles:

Wasted 2 hrs on low-priority emails

Missed gym 3x due to late meetings

Felt distracted Tuesday PM ➔ delayed proposal

3. Decision Accelerator

When: Before critical meetings

Prompt:

"Act as my strategy coach for [decision]:

- 3 options with pros/cons

- Blind spot warning

- Recommended action"

Your Turn: Try This Prompt Right Now

Paste this into ChatGPT and adapt it to your current goal:

```
I'm working on [your project].
Here's what I've written or brainstormed so far:
[paste text or notes]
Help me:
- Clarify my core message
- Spot missing pieces
- Suggest next steps
```

Treat AI as your creative collaborator. You'll be surprised at what you can build–together.

Top AI Prompts List

Use these to think faster, structure better, and gain momentum.

For Clarifying Your Thinking

- "Can you simplify this idea into one sentence?"
- "What's the main point I'm missing here?"
- "Help me break this idea down step by step."

For Organising Complex Content

* "Structure this into 3 clear sections with headings."
* "Turn this brainstorm into a clean outline."
* "Group these ideas into categories."

For Decision-Making

* "List pros/cons of these 3 options."
* "What are the key risks if I choose option A?"
* "What would a strategist recommend here?"

For Writing to Think

* "Ask me 5 questions to help me think clearer about this topic."
* "Help me convert this rough idea into a paragraph I can use."
* "Let's co-create: I'll give you ideas; you expand them one by one."

For Weekly Reflection

* "Here's what happened this week... [paste notes]. What should I repeat or avoid?"
* "Summarise the biggest wins and blockers from this week."
* "Based on this, suggest 3 small goals for next week."

✓ ***Download checklist, tools and templates from https://rahulgoyal.co/resources/ or scan QR code below***

Wrap-Up: The Clarity Principle Behind AI Tools

AI can't think for you – but it can help you think better.

Treat it like a clarity co-pilot.

They're people with **strong questions** and **clear goals**.

AI brings the scaffolding.

You bring the spark.

So, don't wait for AI to become perfect.

Use what's available today–to think better, faster, and clearer.

In our final chapter, we'll build a regular reset habit to stay on track.

Clarity Recap: Chapter 4-6

Chapter 4. The Eisenhower Matrix

- Urgent ≠ Important – they're different.
- Divide tasks into 4 quadrants to decide whether to **Do, Schedule, Delegate**, or **Delete**.
- Mastering this matrix creates focus and long-term progress.

Chapter 5. Calendar Design Thinking

- Don't just use your Calendar – **design** it.
- Time block your most important work.
- Theme your days and protect golden hours.
- Your Calendar should reflect your *strategy*, not your availability.

Chapter 6. AI as a Thinking Partner

- AI isn't here to replace your brain but to support it.
- Use ChatGPT to **structure**, **simplify**, **reflect**, and **create**.
- Give AI context and clear goals – it's your collaborator, not your crutch.

Chapter 7: The Clarity Audit

"When you lose clarity,

You lose momentum."

We don't burn out because we're doing too much. We burn out because we're doing too much of the **wrong** things.

This is where the **Clarity Audit** comes in.

It's not a productivity hack. It's a **strategy ritual**–something you return to monthly or quarterly to clean your mental windshield and refocus. Because the best leaders and creators don't just move fast. They pause to make sure they're moving in the right direction.

Why You Need a Clarity Audit

Life isn't static. Priorities change. Your Calendar fills. Old commitments linger longer than they should.

Without a system to regularly reset, you drift.

A Clarity Audit is your opportunity to:

* Reassess your direction
* Realign your energy
* Rebuild momentum

And you can do it in just 30-60 minutes.

The Clarity Audit Framework

You can run a Clarity Audit monthly, quarterly, or whenever you feel lost in the weeds. Here's how it works:

1. Review: What's Working, What's Not

Take out a notepad or open a fresh doc. Ask:

* **Wins**: What went well lately? What did I enjoy most?
* **Drains**: What felt heavy or unproductive?
* **Gains**: Where did I grow? What stretched me?
* **Misses**: What did I avoid or neglect?

This isn't just journaling. It's intelligence gathering.

2. Refocus: Real Priorities

Look at your goals, projects, and to-dos. Ask:

* "What matters right now?"
* "If I only did 3 things next month, what would they be?"
* "What's noise vs signal?"

Use your answers to trim your goals list.

The goal isn't more – it's less but better.

3. Reset: Energy + Boundaries

Energy is your fuel. Audit it.

- What fuelled me last month?
- What drained me?
- What boundaries do I need to set?
- Where do I need to say no more often?

Use this insight to **protect your Calendar** – and your peace.

4. Refresh: Inputs + Inspiration

Sometimes, feeling stuck is a sign that you need better input. Ask:

- What am I reading/watching/listening to?
- Am I learning or just scrolling?
- Who's in my circle that pushes me to grow?

Refresh your environment, not just your tasks.

The Real ROI of Clarity

People chase tools, routines, and hacks.

But without clarity, everything becomes noise.

A regular Clarity Audit will:

- Help you make better decisions

- Reduce unnecessary stress
- Keep your goals aligned with your growth

Because success isn't about doing more.

It's about doing the right things with the right energy.

✓ ***Download checklist, tools and templates from*** *https://rahulgoyal.co/resources/* ***or scan QR code below***

Wrap-Up: The Clarity Principle Behind the Audit

People chase tools, routines, and hacks. But without clarity, everything becomes noise.

The Clarity Audit brings your attention back to what matters most – before burnout or boredom take over.

* Help you make better decisions
* Reduce unnecessary stress
* Keep your goals aligned with your growth

Because success isn't about doing more.

It's about doing the right things with the right energy.

Your life drifts when you don't review.

Final Clarity Recap

The 7 Tools to Build a Clearer, Smarter Life

Use these tools not all at once but when the moment calls for them. Clarity is a habit–powered by frameworks.

1. The 80/20 Reset

Focus on the vital few.

- 80% of outcomes come from 20% of effort.
- Identify what truly moves the needle–and double down.

2. The ABT Method

Tell better stories.

- Use And, But, Therefore to shape ideas with impact.
- Great communication = action + clarity.

3. The Pyramid Principle

Think top-down like a strategist.

- Start with the answer, then support it with structure.
- Ideal for writing, presenting, and decision-making.

4. The Eisenhower Matrix

Urgent ≠ Important.

- Use 4 quadrants: Do, Schedule, Delegate, Delete.

- Protect long-term goals from short-term noise.

5. Calendar Design Thinking

Design time, don't just manage it.

- Block priority time.
- Theme your days.
- Align Calendar with values, not just tasks.

6. AI as a Thinking Partner

Let AI sharpen–not replace–your brain.

- Use ChatGPT to reflect, plan, and write.
- Great AI use begins with great prompts.

7. The Clarity Audit

Reset regularly.

- What's working, what's not?
- Refresh energy, priorities, and inputs.
- Do this monthly or quarterly for long-term clarity.

Conclusion: Build Your Clarity Stack

You don't need more tools. You need the right tools–used intentionally.

This short book gave you 7 high-leverage frameworks:

- ✳ From business to life
- ✳ From leadership to learning
- ✳ From Calendar to communication

Each tool is:

✅ Simple

✅ Practical

✅ Repeatable

But more than frameworks, what you're building is mental clarity–a deeper understanding of where your energy should go.

What's Next?

Start small. Pick 1 tool that feel most urgent right now. Use them for the next 30 days. See what shifts.

📥 Want to stay updated with more tools, stories, and thinking models? Join me at rahulgoyal.co or subscribe to my newsletter, **JustDraft**.

We're all building our lives with one decision, one habit, and one idea at a time.

This book is your foundation.

Now–go build with clarity.

Resources

A. Clarity Note Template

B. The Clarity Toolkit Checklist

Download checklist, tools and templates from https://rahulgoyal.co/resources/ or scan QR code below

Clarity Note Template

Here's a quick template you can use monthly or quarterly:

🟢 Wins:

🔴 Drains:

📈 Gains:

❌ Misses:

🎯 Top 3 Priorities:

1.
2.
3.

🚫 Things I'm letting go:

🧃 Energy boosters:

🛑 Energy blockers:

📚 What I'm consuming:

👥 Who's inspiring me:

Save it as a shortcut. Run it consistently.

The Clarity Toolkit Checklist

Use this checklist monthly.

1. The 80/20 Reset

[ ] Identify the 20% of work driving results
[ ] Cut or delegate the rest
[ ] Review weekly

2. The ABT Method

[ ] Use AND for context, BUT for tension, THEREFORE for resolution
[ ] Apply it to writing, speaking, presenting

3. The Pyramid Principle

[ ] Start with the answer
[ ] Group ideas and evidence logically
[ ] Write top-down, not bottom-up

4. Eisenhower Matrix

[ ] Use 4 quadrants to sort tasks [Urgent & Important ➔ Do, Not Urgent but Important ➔ Schedule, Urgent but Not Important ➔ Delegate, Neither ➔ Delete]
[ ] Schedule what matters, delete the rest

5. Calendar Design Thinking

[ ] Block deep work
[ ] Theme your days (e.g. Strategy Monday, Admin Friday)
[ ] Add "Buffer zones" for thinking and resets
[ ] Design for energy, not time

6. AI as a Thinking Partner

[ ] Use prompts to clarify and generate ideas
[ ] Reflect, not just automate

7. The Clarity Audit

[ ] Review wins, blocks, and direction
[ ] Refocus goals and habits
[ ] Reset energy and inputs

About the Author

Rahul Goyal is a technology leader and entrepreneur known for spearheading large-scale digital programmes, including the launches of **Jio (India)** and **Rakuten Mobile (Japan)**. He drives **AI and data strategy** for a global telecom leader and is an **award-winning innovator**, recognised as an Airtel Young Achiever and LinkedIn Top Voice in Leadership. Rahul mentors startups across the UK. He shares actionable insights on **AI, leadership, and growth** through his **blog (rahulgoyal.co)** and **newsletter, JustDraft**.

Huma Goyal, Ph.D., is a writer, researcher, and systems thinker who brings clarity to both complex technologies and everyday life. With a doctorate in Electrical Engineering and over a decade leading innovation across India, Japan, and the UK, she has learned that the real breakthroughs–technical or personal–begin with intentional reflection. Her work draws from her journey through high-pressure environments, personal transitions, and a search for a more grounded way to move through the world. Huma lives in Oxford, where she balances tech and matcha, structure and stillness.

9 789334 353723

Printed at Repro India Ltd.